ENTRAÎNEMENT AU TOEIC® LISTENING TEST

Valérie Hanol

À propos de ce cahier

Vous trouverez dans ce cahier des exercices préparatoires, des conseils de méthode et des tests blancs conformes à la certification. Les réponses se trouvent à la fin de chaque test.

Il suffit de vous laisser guider !

Accédez aux enregistrements en flashant ou en photographiant les codes QR avec votre smartphone.

Keep calm and smile!

Vous trouverez après chaque exercice des icônes qui permettront de vous auto-évaluer. En dessinant l'expression de vos icônes, vous pourrez ainsi rapidement identifier les chapitres à retravailler.

Un large sourire 😊 signifie que vous avez tout réussi.

Un sourire « horizontal » 😐 signifie que vous avez obtenu près de 50 % de bonnes réponses.

Une grimace 😟 signifie que le chapitre n'est pas maîtrisé, avec moins de 50 % de bonnes réponses.

Vous trouverez un **tableau d'évaluation** en page 127.

Sommaire

Qu'est-ce que le TOEIC® ?	5
Qu'est-ce que le Listening Test ?	7
Part 1 Photographs	9
Part 2 Questions & responses	41
Part 3 Short conversations	69
Part 4 Short talks	101
Glossaire	123

The Listening test 45 minutes d'épreuve

PART 1	Photographs	6 questions
PART 2	Questions & responses	25 questions
PART 3	Short conversations (with or without visual aid)	39 questions
PART 4	Short talks (with or without visual aid)	30 questions

The Reading test 75 minutes d'épreuve

PART 5	Incomplete sentences	30 questions
PART 6	Complete the text	16 questions
PART 7	Reading / Comprehension	54 questions

Tips (conseils)

- **Essayez de penser en anglais tous les jours** : faites la gymnastique de passer du français à l'anglais. Par exemple, savez-vous dire : Si on allait au cinéma ? La réunion a été annulée ? Si non, faites l'effort de le noter et de chercher la traduction. Constituez votre propre lexique et apprenez-le.

- Voici un site très utile : **www.newsinlevels.com**. Il propose trois niveaux de difficulté pour s'entraîner à la compréhension audio. Je vous recommande le niveau 3, dès le début, car vous y trouverez un script, un audio simplifié et une vidéo.

- **Pour le Reading Test**, entraînez-vous à lire des courriers de correspondances commerciales et soyez au fait du vocabulaire utilisé dans les e-mails professionnels.

Qu'est-ce que le TOEIC® ?

Le TOEIC® (Test of English for International Communication) est une certification qui permet d'**évaluer objectivement votre niveau d'anglais**, indépendamment du cadre scolaire. Le but est donc d'obtenir le score le plus élevé, celui-ci pouvant aller de 10 à 990 points. Bonne nouvelle, il est possible de la passer autant de fois que nécessaire !

Le TOEIC® permet de répondre aux besoins du monde du travail. Il permet de « booster » son C.V. et de se distinguer des autres candidats, quand on convoite un poste à l'international. Bien que cette certification n'ait pas de limite de validité, il est souvent demandé un score récent, allant de 6 mois à 2 ans d'ancienneté.

Le TOEIC® est également **indispensable pour poursuivre certaines études supérieures** : écoles de commerce, d'informatique… Dans les écoles d'ingénieurs, le TOEIC® fait partie des validations de fin d'études. Voici quelques exemples de scores requis par certaines écoles :

- École des mines, 800 points minimum ;
- HEC (École des hautes études commerciales), 800 points minimum ;
- Master de sciences politiques, 900 points minimum.

Tous les ans, 50 millions de certifications sont passées dans le monde.

Pour passer le TOEIC®, il vous en coûtera **entre 61 et 77 euros**.

Se préparer au TOEIC®, c'est s'entraîner comme un sportif, avec des exercices quotidiens. Envisagez-le comme un jeu, ne vous mettez pas la pression : ce n'est pas un examen. Le TOEIC® valorise l'effort et l'on prend du plaisir à avancer, car, une fois rompu à l'exercice, on se rend compte que les thèmes, le vocabulaire et les pièges tendus sont récurrents.

Les thèmes abordés sont ceux de la vie quotidienne (voyages, loisirs, santé…) ou ceux du monde de l'entreprise (finance, achat, correspondance commerciale…). Bonne nouvelle : aucune connaissance de l'actualité n'est requise et les questions sont des Q.C.M.

La certification se déroule habituellement dans un centre d'examen mais elle peut aussi être organisée au sein de votre école ou de votre université.

Quelques contraintes administratives sont à prévoir. Il y a peu de flexibilité dans le choix des dates pour la certification. Les dates de certification sont communes dans tous les centres d'examen en France. Les places sont limitées, alors essayez de vous inscrire suffisamment à l'avance.

Le *D-Day* (le jour J), le test dure **2 heures**, mais prévoyez 3 heures car les formalités prennent au moins 30 minutes.

La certification est composée de **200 questions** également réparties entre le Listening Test et le Reading Test.
- Le Listening Test est composé de 100 questions en Q.C.M. et dure 45 minutes. Il est composé de 4 parties.
- Le Reading Test est aussi composé de 100 questions en Q.C.M. et dure 75 minutes. Il est composé de 3 parties.

Quand vous ferez votre inscription sur Internet, munissez-vous d'une **photo d'identité** que vous scannerez. Pensez à l'apporter le jour de la certification car les photos sont souvent illisibles et l'opération est alors à recommencer. N'oubliez pas vos papiers d'identité !

On vous demandera de **laisser tous vos effets personnels** (sacs, manteaux, téléphones) à l'entrée de la salle, puis vous serez placé et on vous distribuera :
- un livret de questions sur lequel il est interdit d'écrire ;
- un questionnaire plastifié sur lequel il est aussi interdit d'écrire ;
- une feuille avec la grille des réponses à compléter.

Vous devez vous munir d'un crayon à papier, d'une gomme et d'un taille-crayon.

Il convient ensuite de noircir les cases – qui sont des cercles – de la grille de réponses sans dépasser.

> Le TOEIC change en juin 2018. Ce cahier d'entraînement est à jour avec la nouvelle formule !

Qu'est-ce que le Listening Test ?

Le Listening Test est un test de compréhension orale qui comporte 100 questions sous forme de Q.C.M. et est divisé en **4 parties**. Il se déroule en environ **45 minutes**.

Le niveau de difficulté est croissant et demande de la concentration et de la mémoire. Pensez à manger des sucres lents la veille de la certification et des sucres rapides le jour même !

Rappelez-vous que vous ne disposez pas de brouillon ou de feuilles pour prendre des notes.

Voici une présentation générale de ces 4 parties.

• Part 1
Photographs / 6 questions

Vous aurez à votre disposition 6 photographies en noir et blanc sur le livret remis. Quatre réponses vous seront proposées et il n'y a qu'une bonne réponse : A, B, C ou D.

On peut facilement obtenir 6/6 pour cette partie, c'est très encourageant !

• Part 2
Questions & responses / 25 questions

Une question est posée à l'oral et vous entendrez ensuite 3 réponses. Il s'agit de choisir la bonne réponse parmi 3 propositions : A, B ou C.

Attention : pour cette partie, il faut bien connaître les pronoms interrogatifs. Repérez les homonymes et ne tombez pas dans le piège des hallucinations auditives !

45 minutes d'épreuve

• Part 3
Conversations / 39 questions

Dans cette partie, vous entendrez des dialogues et on vous proposera ensuite 4 réponses : A, B, C ou D. Cette partie est longue et nécessite donc une concentration accrue.

Il faut être capable de sélectionner les informations essentielles et il faut faire travailler sa mémoire.

• Part 4
Short talks / 30 questions

Dans cette partie, vous entendrez un seul narrateur vous présenter une situation. Vous aurez le choix ensuite entre 4 réponses : A, B, C ou D. Cette partie est donc la plus difficile d'autant qu'elle suit 30 minutes d'écoute intensive.

Bon à savoir

- On ne peut prendre aucune note et on ne doit rien inscrire sur la grille de réponses en dehors des bonnes réponses.
- On ne peut pas arrêter les enregistrements audio et on ne peut les écouter qu'une fois.
- Il se peut que les accents varient : écossais, indien, asiatique…
- Veillez à ne pas décaler vos réponses, sans quoi c'est le test complet qui sera faux !

Pour cette partie, vous avez sous les yeux une <u>photographie</u> et vous allez <u>entendre quatre propositions</u> de réponses qui décrivent cette photographie en noir et blanc.

Il faudra alors <u>choisir une seule de ces quatre propositions</u> et reporter votre réponse sur votre formulaire de réponse.

Attention, vous n'entendrez <u>qu'une seule fois</u> les quatre réponses.
Dans les conditions de la certification, vous aurez six photographies, nous vous proposons ici trois séries de dix photographies pour que vous puissiez vous entraîner.

Avant chacune de ces séries, vous trouverez <u>quelques mots utiles</u> (qui ne seront bien entendu pas disponibles lors du test) et vous pourrez écouter quelques mots qui ont des prononciations très proches.

 +  →

PART 1 / SÉRIE 1

Série 1

Boîte à outils

- **busy**, *occupé, encombré*
- **congested**, *embouteillé*
- **a hook**, *un hameçon*
- **to land**, *atterrir*
- **loaded**, *chargé*
- **a mechanic**, *un(e) mécanicien(ne)*
- **moored**, *amarré*
- **to push**, *pousser*
- **a screen**, *un écran*
- **a seagull**, *une mouette*
- **to shake**, *serrer, secouer*
- **shaken**, *remué*

Faux-amis auditifs

- **bear**, *supporter*
  ET **bare**, *nu*

- **to be sacked**, *être viré*
  ET **to set**, *installer, disposer*

- **a road**, *une rue*
  ET **a rod**, *une canne à pêche*

Consigne

**Écoutez les quatre propositions audio
et choisissez celle qui correspond le mieux à la photo.**

Voici la consigne telle que vous
l'entendrez lors de la certification.

PART 1 / SÉRIE 1

1 → ....

2 → ....

→ **Voir réponses page 18.**

PART 1 / SÉRIE 1

 → ....

 → ....

→ **Voir réponses page 18.**

PART 1 / SÉRIE 1

5 → .... 🙂

6 → .... 🙂

→ **Voir réponses page 19.**

PART 1 / SÉRIE 1

 → ....

 → ....

→ **Voir réponses page 19.**

PART 1 / SÉRIE 1

 →

 →

→ Voir réponses page 19.

PART 1 / SÉRIE 1 / RÉPONSES

Réponses
de la série 1

a. It's better to give a fishing rod than a fish.
b. **They are holding a fishing rod.**
c. They are on the road.
d. There are plenty of fish in the sea.

a. The seagulls are trapped in the net.
b. **The nets are set over water.**
c. The seagulls are on the net.
d. The flock of seagulls eat sardines.

a. The man has caught two fish.
b. The man is hooked by the fish.
c. The fish is biting the man's hand.
d. **The man caught the fish with a hook.**

a. They are having a coffee.
b. They are shaken.
c. **They are shaking hands.**
d. They are washing their hands.

PART 1 / SÉRIE 1 / RÉPONSES

a. The man is sacked.
b. The man is driving a truck.
c. The man is pushing a sack truck.
d. The boxes are piled up.

a. They are looking at the screen.
b. The man is clicking on the mouse computer.
c. There is a mouse on the computer.
d. They are turning off the screen.

a. He is a mechanic.
b. The woman is wearing a helmet.
c. She is bareheaded.
d. She can't bear wearing a helmet.

a. They're shaking hands.
b. They never applaud.
c. They are applauding the spectacle.
d. They are clapping their hands.

a. The highway is busy.
b. The highway is congested.
c. The trucks are moving in opposite directions.
d. There is heavy traffic.

a. The plane is about to land.
b. The plane is high in the sky.
c. The cargo is loaded.
d. The cargo is moored.

PART 1 / SÉRIE 2

Série 2

Boîte à outils

- **an apron**, *un tablier*
- **crowded**, *plein de monde*
- **cutter pliers**, *pince coupante*
- **to dive**, *plonger*
- **to hike**, *faire de la randonnée*
- **packed**, *rempli*
- **a plug**, *une prise de courant*
- **rush hours**, *heures de pointe*
- **a tie**, *une cravate*
- **a tire**, *un pneu*
- **a waiter**, *un serveur*

Faux-amis auditifs

  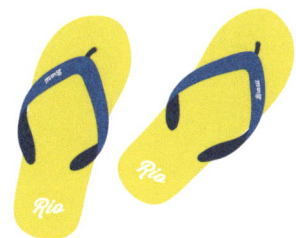

- **tongs**, *pinces*
ET **thongs**, *tongs*

Consigne

**Écoutez les quatre propositions audio
et choisissez celle qui correspond le mieux à la photo.**

PART 1 / SÉRIE 2

→ **Voir réponses page 28.**

PART 1 / SÉRIE 2

 → ....

 → ....

→ **Voir réponses page 28.**

PART 1 / SÉRIE 2

→ Voir réponses page 29.

PART 1 / SÉRIE 2

 → ....

 → ....

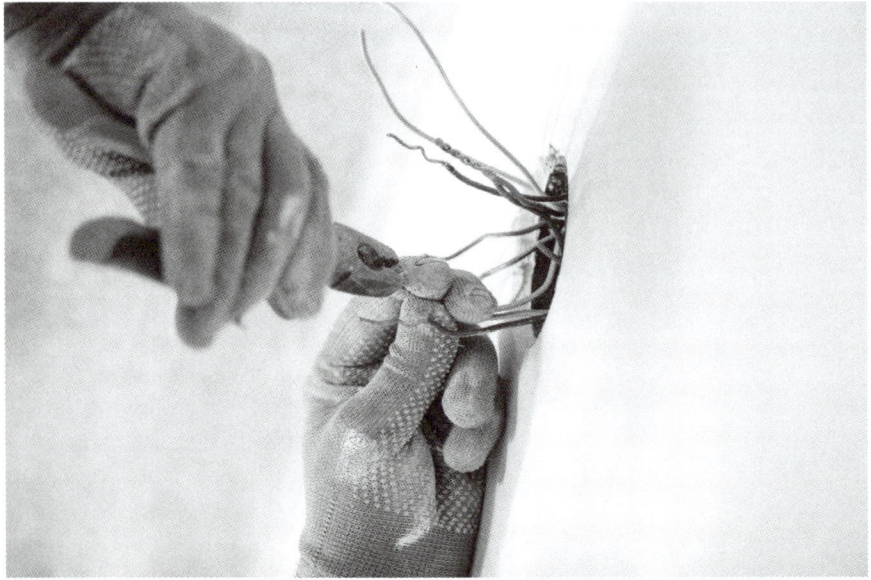

→ **Voir réponses page 29.**

PART 1 / SÉRIE 2

→ **Voir réponses page 29.**

27

Réponses
de la série 2

a. **They are taking the pedestrian crossing.**
b. The pedestrians are cross.
c. The street is empty.
d. They crossed the line.

a. It's rush hour.
b. The street is crowded.
c. **The street is empty.**
d. The street is packed with people.

a. The man is driving.
b. The man is diving.
c. The man is hiking.
d. **The man is riding.**

a. The tables are set for dinner.
b. The restaurant is very crowded.
c. **The lights are on.**
d. The waiters are ready to serve.

PART 1 / SÉRIE 2 / RÉPONSES

 15

a. **The man is wearing an apron.**
b. It's a bike shop.
c. The shop is closed.
d. There are customers.

 16

a. **The man is using tongs.**
b. The man is wearing tongs.
c. The man is wearing thongs.
d. The man is eating.

 17

a. The waiter is waiting.
b. **The waiter is taking an order.**
c. The man is looking at the woman.
d. The waiter is wearing a tie.

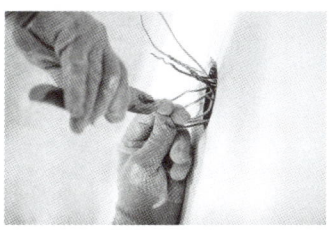

 18

a. The worker is wearing brand new gloves.
b. The worker cut his finger.
c. **The electrician is using cutter pliers.**
d. The electrician is putting his fingers in the plug.

 19

a. The man is tired.
b. The man is eating a pear.
c. **The man is repairing the tire.**
d. The repair drives him mad.

 20

a. **She is using a watering can.**
b. She is planting red roses.
c. The plant is not watered.
d. There is a power plant.

Série 3

Boîte à outils

- **an ATM**, *un distributeur de billets*
- **a bathtub**, *une baignoire*
- **below**, *en dessous*
- **to display**, *disposer*
- **a greengrocer**, *un primeur*
- **a piggy bank**, *une tirelire*
- **a piglet**, *un petit cochon*
- **racket**, *vacarme*
- **rotten**, *pourri*
- **a stable**, *une écurie*
- **a surgery**, *une chirurgie*
- **to undergo**, *subir*
- **a wand**, *une baguette*
- **to withdraw**, *retirer*

Faux-amis auditifs

- **a sink**, *un lavabo*
ET **to sink**, *couler*

Consigne

**Écoutez les quatre propositions audio
et choisissez celle qui correspond le mieux à la photo.**

PART 1 / SÉRIE 3

→ **Voir réponses page 38.**

PART 1 / SÉRIE 3

 → ....

 → ....

→ **Voir réponses page 38.**

PART 1 / SÉRIE 3

 → ....

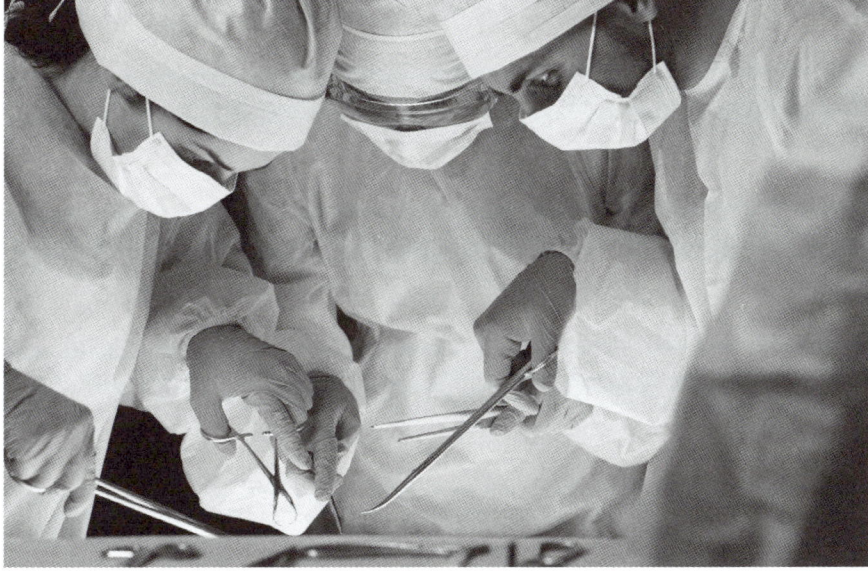

 → ....

→ Voir réponses page 39.

PART 1 / SÉRIE 3

 →

 →

→ **Voir réponses page 39.**

→ Voir réponses page 39.

PART 1 / SÉRIE 3 / RÉPONSES

Réponses
de la série 3

a. The room is tidy.
b. **The place is upside down.**
c. Everything is in its place.
d. The room is not messy.

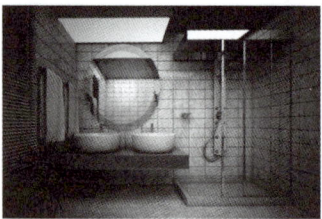

a. The bathtub is very clean.
b. The walls are wooden.
c. **The sinks are below the mirror.**
d. He is sinking into the water.

a. **The athlete is wearing shorts.**
b. He is making a racket.
c. The tennis match is won.
d. He has gone to court.

a. The woman is going into the bank.
b. The man is getting money out of the ATM.
c. No one is waiting.
d. **She is about to withdraw money.**

PART 1 / SÉRIE 3 / RÉPONSES

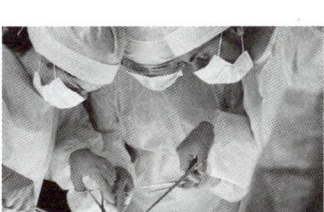

a. The surgeons have a problem.
b. **The patient is undergoing surgery.**
c. They are cutting meat.
d. They are having a meeting.

a. The piglets saw their mum.
b. The big sow is called Piggy.
c. **The sow is breastfeeding.**
d. Piggy banks store money.

a. They are hiking.
b. They are training in the arena.
c. They are in the stables.
d. **They are horse riding outdoors.**

a. The greengrocer only sells tomatoes.
b. The vegetables are rotten.
c. **The vegetables are displayed in wooden crates.**
d. Prices are expensive.

a. They are all using biros.
b. They are in rows.
c. Biros are best.
d. **He is pointing at the document with a biro.**

a. The conductor is holding a magic wand.
b. He is wearing a tie.
c. **He is wearing a bow tie.**
d. The conductor is wearing a hat.

Lors de la certification, pour cette section, il vous sera proposé d'écouter vingt-cinq questions et les trois réponses possibles. Il vous sera alors demandé de cocher la bonne réponse : A, B ou C.

Afin d'aborder au mieux cette partie, nous vous proposons de :
- <u>réviser</u> des notions utiles à ce type d'exercices,
- <u>vous entraîner</u> (*training*) en écoutant la question et les réponses et en vous aidant des scripts écrits que nous vous fournissons,
- vous mettre <u>dans les conditions d'examen</u>, avec l'audio uniquement… et de vérifier vos réponses sur les pages suivantes.

Part 2
Questions & responses

Notions utiles

Les pronoms interrogatifs

Il existe six types de **WH questions**, c'est-à-dire de pronoms interrogatifs commençant par ces deux lettres.

1 **Complétez les lettres manquantes.**

a. Wh......... → Qui

b. Wh......... → Quel(les). Qu'est-ce que…

c. Wh......... → Lequel. Laquelle. Lesquels(les)

d. Wh......... → Pourquoi

e. Wh......... → Où

f. Wh......... → Quand

g. Wh......... → À qui

Les question tags

Certaines questions se présentent aussi sous forme de **question tags**. Dans ce cas, il s'agit d'une affirmation ou d'une confirmation, plutôt que d'une demande réelle d'information.

Your laptop is working, isn't it? I think so. *Votre ordinateur fonctionne, n'est-ce pas ? Il me semble, oui.*

→ Voir réponses page 50.

PART 2 / NOTIONS UTILES

Par ailleurs, de très nombreuses questions commencent par **How**, suivi d'un adjectif.

2 En utilisant les adjectifs suivants, complétez les questions.
deep — far —high — tall — well — old — heavy — fast — big — wide

a. How .... is your suitcase? More than 10 kg.

b. How .... did you understand the exercise? It was alright.

c. How .... is Mount Everest? 8,848 meters.

d. How .... is the pool? More than 2 meters.

e. How .... is your son now? Almost 1m85!

f. How .... are the roads in Scotland? Very narrow.

g. How .... is the nearest petrol station? A few miles away.

h. How .... is this train? The speed can be 380 km/hour.

i. How .... is she? She has just turned 40.

j. How .... is the parcel? It's very voluminous.

Comment traduire Combien ?

How much + singulier ou indénombrable
OU **How many** + pluriel.
How much is it? *Combien ça coûte ?*

→ **Voir réponses page 50.**

PART 2 / NOTIONS UTILES

Comment formuler une question en anglais ?

Attention, en anglais, les questions sont plus souvent structurées sous la forme suivante :

Auxiliaire + sujet + base verbale OU Base verbale + ing

OU participe passé.

- Have you finished?
- Are you working?
- Did you go to the meeting?

Il faut aussi savoir identifier les temps.

Enfin, attention à ne pas tomber dans le piège d'un mot entendu dans la question et dans la réponse. Pour un même mot, il peut y avoir plusieurs significations.

3 Complétez les phrases suivantes avec un pronom interrogatif.

a. .... seems to be the matter with you?

b. .... is the market analysis due?

c. .... came to collect you at the airport?

d. .... would he agree?

e. .... has she been retired?

f. .... office is it?

g. .... calling a meeting?

h. .... people applied for the position?

i. .... did they invest in this merger?

→ **Voir réponses page 50.**

PART 2 / NOTIONS UTILES

4 Complétez les phrases suivantes avec un auxiliaire ou un auxiliaire modal. Faites appel à la grammaire, repérez la forme du verbe.

a. .... the meeting been called off?

b. .... you be able to attend the meting next week?

c. .... Ms Smith going to accept the position?

d. .... you mind explaining the diagram?

e. .... you hold the meeting in Tokyo last month?

f. .... you help me with this new photocopy machine?

g. .... you often go on business trips?

Les homophones

Une des difficultés de l'anglais sont les homophones, c'est-à-dire des mots qui se prononcent de la même façon, mais qui ont une orthographe différente et surtout un sens différent. Seul le contexte pourra vous aider.
Voici quelques exemples d'homophones.
Écoutez la question et choisissez la bonne réponse.

5 Is the meeting at eight?

a. ☐ Yes, we were eight.

b. ☐ Yes, we ate well.

c. ☐ You're right it's at eight.

6 Did you meet the new board?

a. ☐ Not yet.

b. ☐ Yes, I am bored.

c. ☐ Get on board!

→ **Voir réponses page 50.**

PART 2 / NOTIONS UTILES

7 **Have you got some work for me?**

a. ☐ It's a large sum.

b. ☐ Yes, I have some.

c. ☐ Some are for you.

8 **That's a lovely flower, isn't it?**

a. ☐ Yes, I ran out of flour.

b. ☐ As fresh as a daisy!

c. ☐ I prefer roses.

9 **Can you pour me some more?**

a. ☐ Poor me!

b. ☐ No, you've had enough.

c. ☐ There are more poor people.

10 **Have you seen the mail?**

a. ☐ There are more male workers.

b. ☐ I read it.

c. ☐ I will email the document.

11 **Are you joining us for happy hour?**

a. ☐ That's a good idea.

b. ☐ Our CEO is happy.

c. ☐ An hour ago.

➜ **Voir réponses pages 50-51.**

PART 2 / NOTIONS UTILES

12 They're in a conference, aren't they?

a. ☐ There are six.

b. ☐ Their colleagues are sick.

c. ☐ Yes, don't disturb them.

Prenons le « problème » à l'envers !
Retrouvez la question qui a provoqué les réponses suivantes :

13 I will!

a. ☐ Who wants to do the presentation?

b. ☐ Have you made a will?

c. ☐ Did you see the new rep?

14 I am afraid so.

a. ☐ Will you be available next Friday?

b. ☐ When does the bus leave?

c. ☐ Has Paul left already?

15 Speaking!

a. ☐ Do you speak German?

b. ☐ Could I speak to Ms Koshimo?

c. ☐ Can you speak to me please?

→ Voir réponses page 51.

PART 2 / NOTIONS UTILES

16 I could give you a lift.

a. ☐ Can you drive home tomorrow?

b. ☐ Is the lift out of order again?

c. ☐ Can you help me lift this box?

17 An hour ago.

a. ☐ When did he take off?

b. ☐ When is he taking off?

c. ☐ Has he taken off?

18 The end of June.

a. ☐ What will you buy in June?

b. ☐ When is the deadline?

c. ☐ Is June the best time to buy?

→ Voir réponses page 51.

PART 2 / NOTIONS UTILES / RÉPONSES

Réponses
notions utiles

1

a. Who b. What c. Which d. Why e. Where f. When g. Whose

2

a. heavy b. well c. high d. deep e. tall f. wide g. far h. fast i. old j. big

3

a. What b. When c. Who d. Why e. How long f. Which, Whose g. How about h. How many i. How much

4

a. Has b. Will / Would c. Is d. Would e. Did f. Can / Could g. Do

5

c. *L'homophone :* eight / ate.

6

a. *L'homophone :* bored *(ennuyeux)* / board *(comité* ou *à bord d'un bateau)*.

7

b. *L'homophone :* sum / some.

8

c. *L'homophone :* flower *(fleur)* / flour *(farine)*.

9

b. *L'homophone :* poor / pour *(verser)*.

10

b. *L'homophone :* mail *(courrier)* / male *(homme)* / email *(courrier électronique)*.

PART 2 / NOTIONS UTILES / RÉPONSES

11

a. *L'homophone :* our *(notre)* / hour *(heure)*.

12

c. *L'homophone :* They *(ils, elles)* / their *(leur)*.

13

a. I will *exprime l'intention de le faire.*

14

c. I am afraid so = *j'en ai bien peur et non, j'ai peur.*

15

b. Speaking = *c'est moi.*

16

a. To give somebod'y a lift = *déposer quelqu'un en voiture.* A lift = *un ascenseur au Royaume-Uni (aux États-Unis,* elevator*)* / To lift = *soulever.*

17

a. *Prétérit avec* ago.

18

b. Deadline = *date limite.*

Consigne

Voici vingt questions-réponses. Nous vous fournissons ici les scripts pour que vous puissiez vous entraîner en lisant en même temps que vous écoutez les textes. Attention, en conditions d'examen, vous ne pourrez qu'écouter la question et les réponses au choix.

PART 2 / TRAINING

Training

1 **How many employees have been fired?**

a. ☐ They are on fire.

b. ☐ The fire is hot.

c. ☐ Seven all together.

2 **Is the printer out of order again?**

a. ☐ I am afraid it is.

b. ☐ Yes, I passed the order.

c. ☐ Print it again!

3 **Could you give me a lift?**

a. ☐ The lift is out of order.

b. ☐ I can't lift it.

c. ☐ I'd be happy to help!

4 **Does John run a business overseas?**

a. ☐ Yes, he runs fast.

b. ☐ You can see him.

c. ☐ I don't think so.

➜ **Voir réponses page 58.**

PART 2 / TRAINING

 **5** Has the mail arrived yet?

a. ☐ Yes, an hour ago.

b. ☐ Yes, you can read your email.

c. ☐ It's a male director.

 **6** What are the perks of working here?

a. ☐ There is maternity leave.

b. ☐ Long working hours.

c. ☐ I refuse to work overtime.

 **7** When is Bob retiring?

a. ☐ He is very tired.

b. ☐ By the end of May.

c. ☐ He has a plan for his retirement.

 **8** Whose briefcase is it?

a. ☐ It is black.

b. ☐ I don't carry it.

c. ☐ It is Chris's.

 **9** Is the flight to London delayed?

a. ☐ No, the morning flight was on time.

b. ☐ Just by 20 minutes.

c. ☐ I can't stand the delay.

→ **Voir réponses page 58.**

PART 2 / TRAINING

10 Are you on good terms with the CEO?

a. ☐ I'll explain the terms of the contract to her.

b. ☐ Yes, I get along with her.

c. ☐ Shareholders appoint the CEO.

11 Do you have a seating preference for your flight?

a. ☐ Aisle, please.

b. ☐ I don't want to sit.

c. ☐ I prefer flying.

12 How do you spell the CEO's name?

a. ☐ I make spelling mistakes.

b. ☐ I put a spell on him.

c. ☐ Not a clue!

13 He is such a gossip, isn't he?

a. ☐ Yes, she is!

b. ☐ He knows everything that's going on.

c. ☐ Avoid gossips at work.

14 Who attended the lecture?

a. ☐ Practically everyone.

b. ☐ I will attend it.

c. ☐ The lecture was boring.

→ Voir réponses page 59.

PART 2 / TRAINING

15 Has this company gone bankrupt?

a. ☐ The company needs a bank.

b. ☐ Bankruptcies happen.

c. ☐ It might indeed have.

16 How do you do?

a. ☐ How do you do this?

b. ☐ How do you do?

c. ☐ How are you doing?

17 Could you remind me of the deadline?

a. ☐ I am working to a deadline.

b. ☐ We can't meet the deadline.

c. ☐ Monday is the absolute deadline.

18 Do you think the travel expenses will be reimbursed?

a. ☐ No refund!

b. ☐ Travel costs are reasonable.

c. ☐ Compensation and reimbursement are close in meaning.

19 Let's call a meeting, shall we?

a. ☐ I shall see you in the meeting room.

b. ☐ I am packed with meetings.

c. ☐ We shall do this.

→ Voir réponses page 59.

PART 2 / TRAINING

20 Would you agree to telecommute?

a. ☐ Yes, it would be time-saving!

b. ☐ Telecommuting is eco-friendly.

c. ☐ I am a commuter.

➜ Voir réponses page 59.

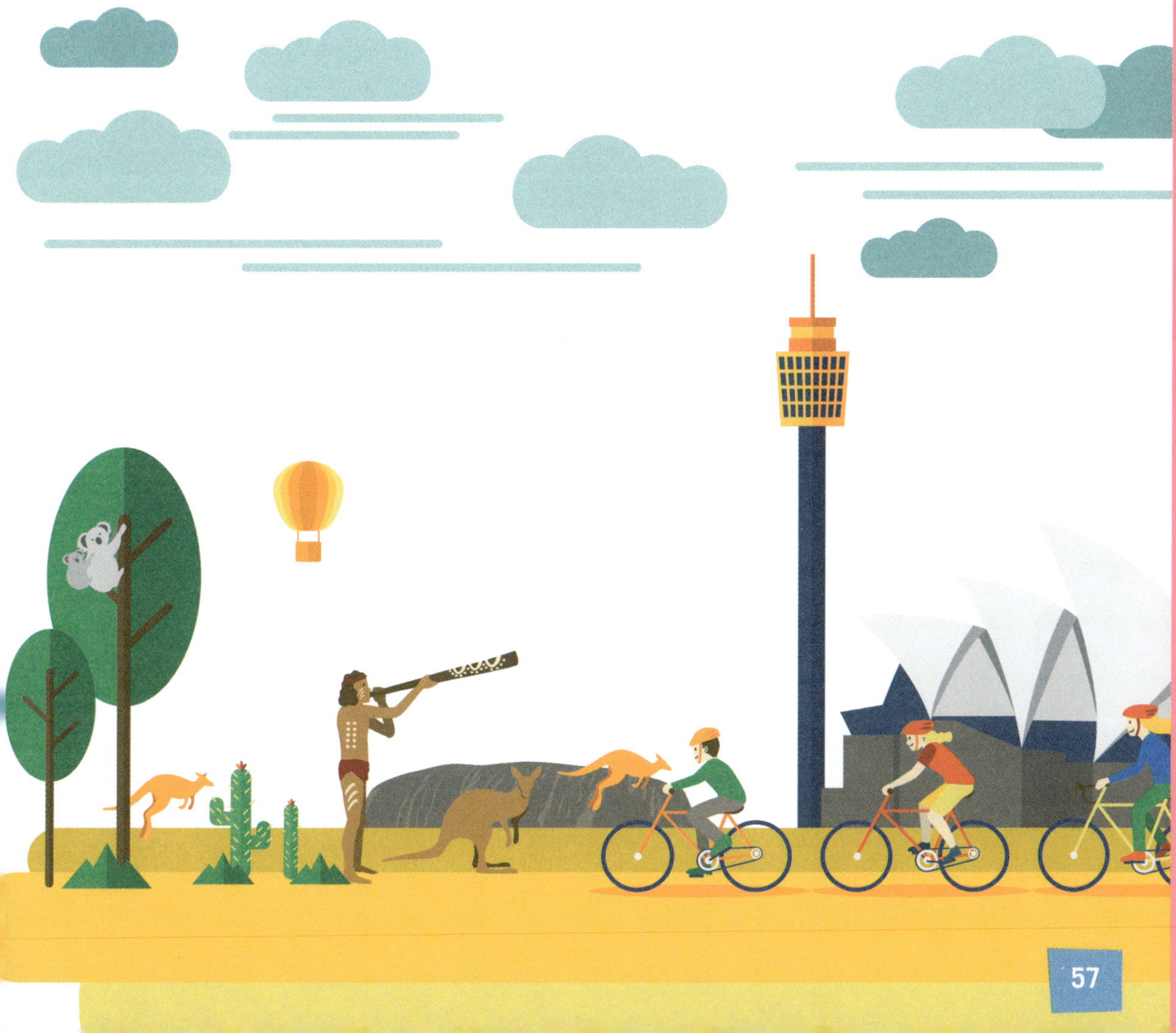

PART 2 / TRAINING / RÉPONSES

Réponses
training

❶

c. Fire = *feu et* get fired = *perdre son travail.*

❷

a. To order = *commander.*

❸

c. Out of order = *hors service*

❹

c. Overseas = *à l'étranger.*

❺

a. The mail = the post.

❻

a. Perks = *avantages en nature.* Maternity leave = *congé maternité.*
Overtime = *heure supplémentaire.*

❼

b. To retire, to be retired, the retirement. *Apprenez ces mots avec toutes les classes grammaticales.*

❽

c. *Attention à la prononciation du génitif (cas possessif) quand le mot se termine par un s. Par exemple,* James's, Alexis's s*e prononcent iz en fin de mot.*

❾

b. *La réponse* **a.** *ne convient pas à cause du temps.* I can't stand = *je ne peux pas supporter.*

PART 2 / TRAINING / RÉPONSES

b. CEO = chief executive officer = *PDG*. To appoint = *nommer*. Shareholder = *actionnaire*.

a. *Attention à la prononciation de* sit *et* seat.

c. Spelling mistake = *faute d'orthographe*. To put a spell = *ensorceler*. I don't have clue = *je n'en ai pas la moindre idée*.

b. Gossip = *commérage*.

a. To attend = *assister à*. A lecture = *un cours, une conférence*.

c. To go bankrupt = *faire faillite*. The bankrupcy = *la banqueroute*.

b. *À la question*, How do you do? *on répond la même chose !* *C'est le synonyme de :* pleased to meet you.

c. *La réponse* **a.** *est : J'ai un délai à respecter et* **b.** *: On ne peut pas respecter les délais.*

a.

c. *La réponse* **b.** *est : Je vais de réunion en réunion.*

a. To commute = *travailler depuis chez soi*.

Consigne

Voici vingt questions-réponses, telles qu'elles vous seront proposées le jour du test. Écoutez et entourez la bonne réponse. Notez que l'on vous en proposera vingt-cinq du même type lors de la certification.

Voici la consigne telle que vous l'entendrez lors de la certification.

PART 2 / EN CONDITIONS D'EXAMEN

En conditions d'examen

 **1**
- a. ☐
- b. ☐
- c. ☐

 **2**
- a. ☐
- b. ☐
- c. ☐

 **3**
- a. ☐
- b. ☐
- c. ☐

 **4**
- a. ☐
- b. ☐
- c. ☐

 **5**
- a. ☐
- b. ☐
- c. ☐

 **6**
- a. ☐
- b. ☐
- c. ☐

 **7**
- a. ☐
- b. ☐
- c. ☐

 **8**
- a. ☐
- b. ☐
- c. ☐

➜ Voir réponses pages 64-65.

PART 2 / EN CONDITIONS D'EXAMEN

a. ☐
b. ☐
c. ☐

a. ☐
b. ☐
c. ☐

a. ☐
b. ☐
c. ☐

a. ☐
b. ☐
c. ☐

a. ☐
b. ☐
c. ☐

a. ☐
b. ☐
c. ☐

a. ☐
b. ☐
c. ☐

a. ☐
b. ☐
c. ☐

a. ☐
b. ☐
c. ☐

a. ☐
b. ☐
c. ☐

→ Voir réponses pages 65-67.

PART 2 / EN CONDITIONS D'EXAMEN

 **19**

a. ☐

b. ☐

c. ☐

 **20**

a. ☐

b. ☐

c. ☐

→ Voir réponses page 67.

PART 2 / EN CONDITIONS D'EXAMEN / RÉPONSES

Réponses
de cette mise en conditions

① What time does the express leave?

a. It is a midnight express.

b. In a quarter of an hour.

c. It leaves rapidly.

② Did you check the order?

a. I will draw a check.

b. Your wish is my command.

c. Everything is in order. (To order = *commander*.)

③ Were you not supposed to be on a business trip?

a. I did good business.

b. I returned yesterday. (To trip over = *trébucher*.)

c. I often trip up.

④ How about trying this new fish restaurant?

a. That's another kettle of fish. (= *C'est une autre paire de manches.*)

b. I have other fish to fry. (= *J'ai d'autres chats à fouetter.*)

c. Sorry, I am allergic to iodine.

PART 2 / EN CONDITIONS D'EXAMEN / RÉPONSES

5 Have you ever gone skydiving?

a. No, I can't dive.

b. Yes, the sky was blue.

c. **No, I wish I could. (Skydiving = *parachutisme*.)**

6 How much did you pay for it?

a. **An awful lot.**

b. It was a big fat paycheck. (A paycheck = *un salaire*.)

c. I will pay £150.

7 Will Ms Lee be attending the lecture?

a. No, we've been lecturing her.

b. **No, she won't. (To attend = *assister à*.)**

c. No, he won't.

8 There isn't enough room for all of us, is there?

a. There are only three rooms.

b. We all have a room.

c. **Don't worry it's roomy. (Room = *place* ; roomy = *spacieux*.)**

9 Did you find the training helpful?

a. **To a degree.**

b. I train quite often.

c. No, the train was late.

10 Why is John leaving the company?

a. She lives in London.

b. **Not a clue.**

c. Yes, the company is leaving.

65

PART 2 / EN CONDITIONS D'EXAMEN / RÉPONSES

 John has no IT skills, has he?

a. **No, he studied languages.**

b. He has to be skilful.

c. John hit his computer.

 Do you dye your roots?

a. My hair is dying.

b. The roots are deep.

c. **Yes, my roots are white.**

 Can you lend me your laptop, please?

a. Yes, come on my lap.

b. **No, my laptop crashed.**

c. Yes, there is one lap to go.

 Mustn't you get your car serviced?

a. **Yes, it is high time.**

b. Yes, the service is included.

c. Services are not required.

 Can you call the rep for me please?

a. Yes, he called for you.

b. **I shall do it.**

c. Please, call again.

 Has somebody turned off the heating?

a. **Not me!**

b. It heats up quicker.

c. It will soon be time to turn it up.

PART 2 / EN CONDITIONS D'EXAMEN / RÉPONSES

17. Shouldn't you ask your certified public accountant?

a. Accountants are absolutely necessary.

b. **I always ask my CPA. (CPA = certified public accountant. To sign off on something = *valider*.)**

c. Accountants sign off on the accounts.

18. Do you keep a correct ledger book?

a. No, I am not a bookkeeper.

b. **All funds are recorded, of course. (Bookkeeper = *comptable*. To record = *enregistrer*.)**

c. No, it's not correct.

19. Is it correct to say 'I am agree'?

a. We agree with this.

b. I agree on the choice.

c. **No! That's a huge mistake.**

20. Are you going to apply for the job?

a. **I fit the job requirements.**

b. I have to apply for a job.

c. Redo your profile to apply for a job.

Lors de la certification, pour cette partie, vous entendrez treize conversations entre deux ou trois personnes. Elles tournent habituellement autour de thèmes de la vie quotidienne et professionnelle, littéralement de la pluie et du beau temps ! Chaque conversation est assez courte (environ 100 mots). Certains textes (trois sur treize) vous seront proposés avec une aide visuelle, c'est-à-dire un document écrit qui se trouve avant les questions.
Vous seront ensuite proposées trois questions avec un choix entre quatre réponses pour chaque. Il y a une seule bonne réponse.

Afin d'aborder au mieux cette partie, nous vous proposons de :
- <u>travailler votre écoute et votre mémoire</u> sur six conversations entre un homme et une femme. Ne vous déconcentrez pas. Les dialogues sont courts et l'essentiel est dit rapidement. Les trois questions suivent l'ordre du texte. Soyez attentifs aux dates, aux chiffres, aux nombres, aux couleurs, aux prix... Les lieux sont rarement mentionnés,
- <u>repérer les mots-clefs</u> et les informations pertinentes dans des conversations,
- vous mettre <u>dans les conditions d'examen</u>, avec l'audio et les aides visuelles uniquement... et de vérifier vos réponses sur les pages suivantes.

Faites attention au développement dans les dialogues : il y a souvent un mini-problème auquel on essaie de trouver une solution.

Part 3
Short conversations

Consigne

Pour commencer à exercer votre mémoire, écoutez ces dialogues très courts et répondez aux questions.

PART 3 / TRAINING

Training

1

Man: Mary, you look cross! What's the matter?

Woman: Jim got the promotion instead of me!

Man: But he has less experience than you have. Only 2 years!

Woman: Yes, that's why I am thinking of suing the company.

Questions

a. Why is Mary angry?

→ ....
....

b. How long has Jim been working?

→ ....
....

c. What does Mary intend to do?

→ ....
....

→ **Voir réponses page 77.**

PART 3 / TRAINING

Woman: Oh no! The copier broke down again.

Man: It's the second time this week. Let's call maintenance.

Woman: We'd better change brand.

Questions

a. What's the problem?

→ ....

b. Does it happen often?

→ ....

c. What does the woman suggest?

→ ....

→ **Voir réponses page 77.**

Man: Look at John's school report!

Woman: Oh gosh! It has never been worse! What shall we do?

Man: No more video games, no outings with friends.

Questions

a. What have the parents received?

➔ ....
....

b. Has John got good marks?

➔ ....
....

c. What will the parents do?

➔ ....
....

➔ **Voir réponses page 77.**

PART 3 / TRAINING

Woman: I can't believe what I heard! You swore at the marketing manager!

Man: I didn't mean it really! It just slipped out. I hope he won't hold it against me!

Woman: You must be joking! He's going to fire you!

Questions

a. What did the man do?

→ ....
....

b. Did the manager hear that he swore at him?

→ ....
....

c. What is going to happen next?

→ ....
....

→ **Voir réponses page 77.**

PART 3 / TRAINING

5

Man: Excuse me officer, where is my car?

Officer: It has been towed away because it was a car park reserved for disabled people.

Man: Oh come on! Everybody does it!

Officer: And on top of that you'll get a $90 fine.

Questions

a. Where is the man's car?

→ ....
....

b. Why?

→ ....
....

c. How much will he be charged?

→ ....
....

→ **Voir réponses page 77.**

PART 3 / TRAINING

Woman: Can you please lower the volume?

Man: But it's my favourite band!

Woman: Stop that, I have to focus on the road.

Man: Yes, you'd better be careful because you've just run a red light!

Questions

a. Where are the two speakers?

→ ....
....

b. Why doesn't the man want to turn the music down?

→ ....
....

c. What did the woman do?

→ ....
....

→ **Voir réponses page 77.**

PART 3 / TRAINING / RÉPONSES

Réponses
training

1
a. Because she didn't get the promotion. b. 2 years c. Sue the company.

2
a. The copier is out of order. b. Yes, twice a week. c. To switch brand.

3
a. John's school report. b. Never been so bad. c. John will be grounded.

4
a. He insulted the marketing manager. b. Yes, he did. c. The man is going to lose his job.

5
a. At a vehicle pound. b. Because he parked on a car park reserved for disabled persons. c. A $90 fine.

6
a. In a car. b. It's his favourite band. c. A driving infraction.

Consigne

Écoutez les documents audio et repérez les mots-clés et informations pertinentes pour les réutiliser afin de répondre aux questions.

PART 3 / TRAINING

Woman: The parking lot is closed so I had to park at the mall and they are charging me $4 an hour. I can't believe it!

Man: You shouldn't complain about it because most places charge more than that, up to $6. At least we won't miss the beginning of the film.

Woman: When does it start?

Man: In about 8 minutes. Let's walk faster because if we miss the beginning of the plot we won't understand the rest of the film.

Mots-clés et informations pertinentes
- A mall (shopping center)   ○ A parking lot (a car park)
- The plot (the story line)   ○ To charge (price asked)

Questions

1. Where did the woman park the car?

a. ○ In the garage.   b. ○ At her office.
c. ○ In the mall's parking lot.   d. ○ At home.

2. How much do they charge her?

a. ○ $3.   b. ○ $4.   c. ○ $5.   d. ○ $6.

3. Where are the speakers going?

a. ○ To a concert.
b. ○ To a basketball match.
c. ○ To the cinema.
d. ○ To work.

→ **Voir réponses page 84.**

PART 3 / TRAINING

Woman: This is the most boring conference I have ever attended. I almost fell asleep!

Man: I totally agree, I learned nothing and wasted some precious time. I have a lot on my plate these days at work.

Woman: Well, next time, I'll attend the meeting through a videoconference and I shall make a summary for you.

Man: Thank you, I really appreciate that. I owe you!

Mots-clés et informations pertinentes
◯ Boring meeting ◯ Videoconference next time ◯ Do a favour

Questions

1. How did they both react at the meeting?

a. ◯ They had a good time.   b. ◯ They slept.
c. ◯ They listened closely.   d. ◯ They were deadly bored.

2. What does the woman intend to do?

a. ◯ To send her apologies.   b. ◯ To send her colleague.
c. ◯ Not to attend the next conference.
d. ◯ To attend the next conference through a video.

3. What will the man do next time?

a. ◯ Do her the same favor.   b. ◯ He will prepare the conference.
c. ◯ He will make a video.   d. ◯ He won't make a summary.

→ **Voir réponses page 84.**

PART 3 / TRAINING

Woman: John you look down, what's happening?

Man: I am afraid I'll be jobless again.

Woman: But you started 2 months ago!

Man: That's the point, the company will implement mass redundancies. Last in, first out.

Mots-clés et informations pertinentes
○ The man is sad (down)   ○ Jobless (unemployed)
○ To make redanduncies (to fire the workforce, to lay off)

Questions

1. Why is the man sad?

a. ☐ Because he got the job.   b. ☐ Because he will be laid off.

c. ☐ Because he has worked hard for 2 months.

d. ☐ Because he came first.

2. How long ago did he start?

a. ☐ 2 years ago.   b. ☐ 4 months ago.

c. ☐ 2 months ago.   d. ☐ Last month.

3. Why will he be laid off?

a. ☐ The man didn't fit the job.

b. ☐ Because he arrived last.

c. ☐ He was late at work.

d. ☐ It was his first job.

→ **Voir réponses page 84.**

PART 3 / TRAINING

Woman: You look exhausted this morning!

Man: I didn't get a wink!

Woman: Why so?

Man: Baby Jenny coughed all night and had a temperature. We eventually called the doctor.

Woman: How is she now?

Man: Resting comfortably.

Mots-clés et informations pertinentes
○ Exhausted (very tired) ○ To cough (*tousser*)

Questions

1. Why is the man exhausted?

a. ○ His wife had a baby.   b. ○ He rested.

c. ○ He had a sleepless night.   d. ○ He coughed all night.

2. What was wrong with the baby?

a. ○ She was resting.   b. ○ She was in good shape.

c. ○ Her tummy hurt.   d. ○ She hag a cough.

3. Who was called?

a. ○ 999.   b. ○ A physician.

c. ○ A chemist.   d. ○ A nurse.

→ Voir réponses page 84.

PART 3 / TRAINING

Man: Look at those big black clouds! Do you think we'll be able to have David's retirement party in the park?

Woman: I checked the weather forecast. There will be light rain showers.

Man: Are you sure? Because it looks like it's going to rain cats and dogs.

Woman: Come on! You're such a killjoy!

Mots-clés et informations pertinentes
○ Black sky rain   ○ No problem   ○ Pessimistic man

Questions

1. What kind of celebration will take place?

a. ☐ David's birthday.   b. ☐ The cat's birthday.
c. ☐ David's promotion.   d. ☐ A retirement party.

2. What's the weather like?

a. ☐ The sky is black.   b. ☐ The sun is shining.
c. ☐ It's stormy.   d. ☐ It's snowy.

3. What is the man's mood?

a. ☐ He is grumpy.
b. ☐ Cheerful.
c. ☐ Overjoyed.
d. ☐ He is pessimistic.

Aide visuelle exercice 11

➜ **Voir réponses page 84.**

PART 3 / TRAINING / RÉPONSES

Réponses
training

7
1. c. **2.** b. **3.** c.

8
1. d. **2.** d. **3.** a.

9
1. b. **2.** c. **3.** b.

10
1. c. **2.** d. **3.** b.

11
1. d. **2.** a. **3.** d.

Consigne

Nous vous proposons dix questions et leurs réponses telles qu'elles vous seront posées le jour de l'examen. Vous en aurez alors trente-neuf. Écoutez les dialogues, puis les questions et les réponses proposées. Pour certains exercices, une aide visuelle permet d'obtenir des indices. Sélectionnez ensuite la bonne réponse.

Voici la consigne telle que vous l'entendrez lors de la certification.

PART 3 / EN CONDITIONS D'EXAMEN

En conditions d'examen

 **1** 😊

1. a.☐ b.☐ c.☐ d.☐
2. a.☐ b.☐ c.☐ d.☐
3. a.☐ b.☐ c.☐ d.☐

 **2** 😊

1. a.☐ b.☐ c.☐ d.☐
2. a.☐ b.☐ c.☐ d.☐
3. a.☐ b.☐ c.☐ d.☐

 **3** 😊

1. a.☐ b.☐ c.☐ d.☐
2. a.☐ b.☐ c.☐ d.☐
3. a.☐ b.☐ c.☐ d.☐

 **4** 😊

1. a.☐ b.☐ c.☐ d.☐
2. a.☐ b.☐ c.☐ d.☐
3. a.☐ b.☐ c.☐ d.☐

 **5** 😊

1. a.☐ b.☐ c.☐ d.☐
2. a.☐ b.☐ c.☐ d.☐
3. a.☐ b.☐ c.☐ d.☐

 **6** 😊

1. a.☐ b.☐ c.☐ d.☐
2. a.☐ b.☐ c.☐ d.☐
3. a.☐ b.☐ c.☐ d.☐

Aide visuelle exercice 5

TRAIN TICKET

CLASS	TICKET TYPE	ADULT	CHILD
STD	SINGLE	ONE	NIL

ARRIVE LONDON
DEPARTURE MANCHESTER
DATE 07/06
PRICE £15.30

LND-MSC-0706-1430-07B

TRAIN TICKET

CLASS	DATE
STD	07/06
SEAT	HOUR
07-B	14:30

LND-MSC-0706
1430-07B

➜ **Voir réponses pages 89-93.**

PART 3 / EN CONDITIONS D'EXAMEN

1. a.☐ b.☐ c.☐ d.☐

2. a.☐ b.☐ c.☐ d.☐

3. a.☐ b.☐ c.☐ d.☐

1. a.☐ b.☐ c.☐ d.☐

2. a.☐ b.☐ c.☐ d.☐

3. a.☐ b.☐ c.☐ d.☐

1. a.☐ b.☐ c.☐ d.☐

2. a.☐ b.☐ c.☐ d.☐

3. a.☐ b.☐ c.☐ d.☐

1. a.☐ b.☐ c.☐ d.☐

2. a.☐ b.☐ c.☐ d.☐

3. a.☐ b.☐ c.☐ d.☐

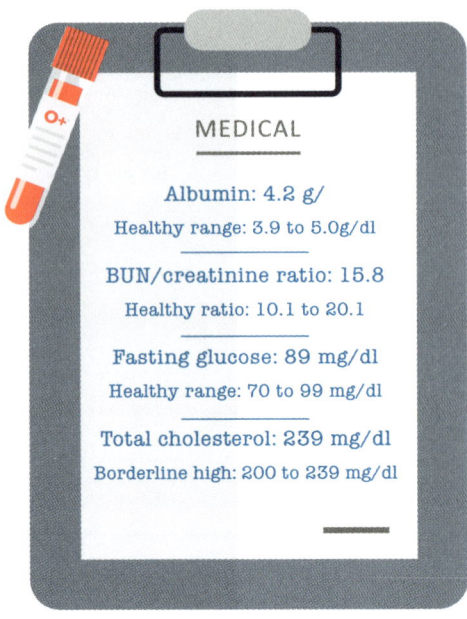

Aide visuelle exercice 7

➡ **Voir réponses pages 95-98.**

PART 3 / EN CONDITIONS D'EXAMEN / RÉPONSES

Réponses
de cette mise en conditions

Woman: Peter and I are going to that new Chinese restaurant. Do you want to come along?

Man: You mean the one on Baker Street? I wish I could, but I tried it last week and the service was pretty slow. I don't have much time for lunch today.

Woman: Well, we'll see, maybe they needed some time to adjust. You should come with us and if you run out of time, you can always skip the dessert!

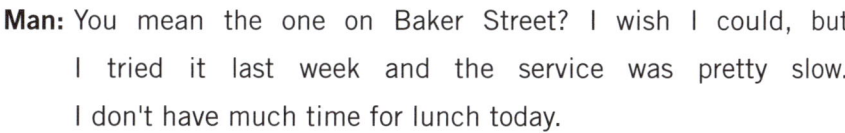

Questions

1. What are the speakers discussing?

a. A problem at work.   **b.** A problem of timing.
c. A new restaurant.   **d.** The Chinese economy.

2. When did the man go to the place being discussed?

a. A week ago.   **b.** Last month.   **c.** Last summer.   **d.** A long time ago.

3. What will the man have to do if he decides to join his colleagues?

a. Work harder.   **b.** Skip the main course.
c. Skip the starter.   **d. Forget about the sugary treats.**

PART 3 / EN CONDITIONS D'EXAMEN / RÉPONSES

Man: I have looked and checked my hotel room, but my mobile phone is nowhere. It's a total disaster because I have all my contacts on it and I haven't saved them!

Woman: Keep calm Robbie, have you checked the auditorium where we had the effective training strategies?

Man: No I haven't! If only that were true! I am on my way.

Questions

1. What is the man looking for?

a. His hotel room.
b. His computer.
c. **His portable telephone.**
d. His colleague.

2. Why is he so concerned about the lost object?

a. Because it was expensive.
b. **Because it contains valuable data.**
c. Because there are photos.
d. Because the battery is dead.

3. Where is the man going to look for it?

a. **In a conference room.**   b. In his car.
c. In his hotel.   d. In his contact list.

PART 3 / EN CONDITIONS D'EXAMEN / RÉPONSES

Man: Hello Mrs Harris, this is James Connors from Scrooge bank. I am calling you to verify some unusual activity on your credit card account.

Woman: Oh gosh, what kind of activity? Should I be worried?

Man: Well Mrs Harris I just wanted to confirm 3 large transactions in dollars posted in New York.

Woman: Oh yes, we bought 3 pieces of furniture for our daughter.

Questions

1. Who most likely is the man?

a. A thief.   **b.** A policeman.   **c. A banker.**   **d.** A seller of furniture.

2. What is the purpose of the call?

a. To check she has sufficient funds.
b. To rob her money.
c. To verify a transaction on her account.
d. To buy furniture.

3. What does the woman tell the man?

a. Everything is in order.
b. She wants to make a money order.
c. She has got a son.
d. To close her account.

PART 3 / EN CONDITIONS D'EXAMEN / RÉPONSES

Woman: I was wondering if we had received the contract from Ms Smith? She was supposed to email it today.

Man: Nothing has arrived yet. If we don't get it at noon, I'll call her.

Woman: Yes, you should phone her just to be on the safe side. But I wouldn't worry because you can rely on her.

Questions

1. When does the conversation take place?

a. At noon.
b. In the afternoon.
c. Before noon.
d. At night.

2. What are they waiting for?

a. Nothing.   b. An email.   c. A letter.   d. A fax.

3. What kind of person is Ms Smith?

a. She is reliable.
b. You can't trust her.
c. She is not trustworthy.
d. She is erratic.

PART 3 / EN CONDITIONS D'EXAMEN / RÉPONSES

Woman: Morning, could I have a single to Manchester for today please?

Man: What time do you want to leave? You can take the express at 10:15 or take the 13:05 with a stop in Warrington.

Woman: I would rather travel on a direct train. How much is it?

Man: It's £15.30 and it departs from platform 3 in 30 minutes. Have a good journey!

Questions

1. Where does the scene take place?

a. At a coach station.

b. At a train station.

c. At the airport.

d. At an underground station.

2. What kind of ticket does the woman want?

a. A return ticket.   **b. A one-way ticket.**

c. Two single tickets.   d. Two return tickets.

3. How much is a ticket?

a. £10.15.

b. £13.05.

c. £15.30.

d. £30.

PART 3 / EN CONDITIONS D'EXAMEN / RÉPONSES

Man: I think we'll soon run out of T-shirts and the product is out of stock. I had better call our supplier and ask for 50 more.

Woman: Don't you think we should order a hundred more to reduce the shipping costs?

Man: You're right, with the annual summer sale starting next month, business should be on the rise and the T-shirts will sell like wildfire.

Questions

1. What are the speakers discussing?

a. Their summer holidays.
b. The business failure.
c. A fashionable T-shirt.
d. A new order.

2. When will the yearly summer sale begin?

a. Next week.   b. In the fall.   c. Next month.   d. In two months.

3. What will the man do?

a. Order 50 more T-shirts.
b. Wait till next month.
c. Ask for a special price.
d. Order a hundred T-shirts.

PART 3 / EN CONDITIONS D'EXAMEN / RÉPONSES

Man: Hello Doctor Quinn, have you received the results of my blood test?

Woman: Yes, the laboratory has just sent them back. Well, almost everything looks fine.

Man: Almost everything? What's wrong?

Woman: You are in a good healthy state, but your rate of cholesterol is borderline. And I have specific recommendations: you should go on a low fat diet and get exercise.

Man: Ok then, I shall do that! I'll try to work on that before our next appointment in 6 months.

Questions

1. Where does the conversation take place?

a. In a laboratory.   **b.** At the vet's.
c. At the drugstore.   **d. At the doctor's.**

2. Why should the man exercise?

a. Because his blood sugar level is high.
b. Because he works too much.   **c.** Because he is too fat.
d. Because he has cholesterol.

3. When will the man probably return?

a. Never.   **b. In 6 months time.**   **c.** In 3 months.   **d.** The next day.

PART 3 / EN CONDITIONS D'EXAMEN / RÉPONSES

Man: Did you hear the news? The famous rock singer Johnny Day has died.

Woman: Seriously? How come? I saw him in a concert three weeks ago and he looked in good shape. What a shock!

Man: Actually he had a condition he kept hidden from his fans.

Woman: Well I think he will be honored with a national tribute because he was a legend!

Questions

1. What is the breaking news?

a. A actor died.   **b.** A politician died.

c. A rock star died.   **d.** A concert is cancelled.

2. Why has it come as a surprise?

a. Because his fans didn't know he was sick.

b. Because he was young.

c. Because he was unseen.

d. Because he fell between the cracks.

3. What kind of funeral will be organized?

a. An intimate setting.   **b.** A modest ceremony.

c. A secret ceremony.   **d. A state funeral.**

PART 3 / EN CONDITIONS D'EXAMEN / RÉPONSES

Man: Can I get your order Madam?

Woman: Yes, but can you tell me what your specials are today?

Man: As a starter you have a choice between a shrimp salad or a rice salad as for the main course it is either scallops or a T-bone with French beans. The dessert is a cheesecake.

Woman: Well, I'll have a shrimp salad and scallops but could I have rice instead of green beans because I don't like them.

Man: I'll ask the chef if it's possible.

Questions

1. Where is the woman?

a. At the canteen.   **b.** At the staff cafeteria.

c. At home.   **d. At the restaurant.**

2. What doesn't she like?

a. Cheese.   **b.** Beef.   **c. French beans.**   **d.** Rice.

3. Who is the waiter going to ask?

a. The cook.

b. The boss.

c. The wine expert.

d. The maid.

PART 3 / EN CONDITIONS D'EXAMEN / RÉPONSES

Man: The future homeowner has just called to know if he could come and see the progress of the work.

Woman: Does he want to see both the inside and the outside because I won't be able to stay more than an hour because I have an appointment at 3 pm with the town hall officials.

Man: I think he just wants to have an overview of the premises. It shouldn't take long.

Woman: Then tell him to come at 1:30 pm sharp and make sure he knows I can't spare him much time.

Questions

1. Who most likely is the woman?

a. A contractor.   **b. An architect**.   **c.** A builder.   **d.** The mayor.

2. When will the owner arrive?

a. At 3 pm.   **b.** After 13:30.

c. At 13:30 precisely.   **d.** In an hour.

3. Why doesn't the woman have much time?

a. Because she is slow.

b. Because the works are delayed.

c. Because she has another appointment.

d. Because she doesn't want to justify herself.

Lors de la certification, pour cette partie, vous entendrez dix audios avec un seul locuteur. Les textes sont courts (environ 100 mots). Cette session ne présente pas de difficultés particulières, mais elle suit les parties 1, 2 et 3… L'oreille est, certes, exercée mais vos capacités d'attention et de concentration seront probablement un peu réduites. Courage !
Stay focused!

Certains textes vous seront proposés avec une aide visuelle, c'est-à-dire un document écrit qui se trouve avant les questions.

Les textes, une fois encore, traitent de sujets de la vie de tous les jours et professionnelle : faites appel à vos connaissances et à votre logique.

Vous seront ensuite proposées trois questions à l'oral avec un choix entre quatre réponses écrites pour chaque. Il y a une seule bonne réponse.

Part 4
Short talks

Consigne

Avec les exercices qui suivent, vous allez travailler le repérage rapide des informations. Écoutez le texte et les questions, puis choisissez la bonne réponse parmi les propositions données.

Training

If you have never used an online bank you may wonder what the experience is like. What makes them different from the bank you currently use? There are plenty of similarities but a few differences make online banks especially attractive.

First, it's perfect for those who want 24.7 access to their funds and who want to conduct their banking business anywhere.

Secondly, online banks are known for paying higher interest rates as you don't have to pay overhead costs.

Last but not least, you go paperless which is eco-friendly!

Boîte à outils

- **currently,** *actuellement*
- **interest rates,** *taux d'intérêts*
- **overhead costs,** *frais généraux*
- **paperless,** *dématérialisé*
- **eco-friendly,** *respectueux de l'environnement*

PART 4 / TRAINING

 (suite)

Questions

1. Why are online banks attractive?

a. ☐ They are nice.   **b.** ☐ They are easy to use.

c. ☐ You don't need a computer.

d. ☐ They are similar to regular banks.

2. When can you use online bank services?

a. ☐ During business days.   **b.** ☐ Only at weekends.

c. ☐ 12 hours a day.   **d.** ☐ Anytime.

3. Why are they worth it?

a. ☐ You get better interest rates.   **b.** ☐ They are polluting.

c. ☐ They are expensive.   **d.** ☐ You get the services from the teller.

❷

Before you even begin salary negociations with a prospective employer, you need to find out how much the job is worth, and how much your skills and experience are worth to the employer.

The most productive salary negociations occur between people who realize that they have a common goal. Negociations needn't be adversarial and no one has to get aggresive. The rule of thumb is to take it slowly.

Negociations can include all aspects of compensation, including salary, bonuses, stock option benefits, perks and vacation time.

→ **Voir réponses page 108.**

PART 4 / TRAINING

 **(suite)**

Boîte à outils

- **to be worth,** *montrer ce que l'on vaut*
- **skills,** *compétences*
- **a rule of thumb,** *en règle générale*
- **compensation,** *remboursement des frais*
- **bonus,** *prime*
- **perks,** *avantages sociaux*
- **commuting,** *télétravail*

Questions

1. What must you show your employer?

a. ☐ You are quick.   b. ☐ You are a warrior.
c. ☐ You are worth being hired.   d. ☐ You are not worthy.

2. How should you behave?

a. ☐ Be offensive.   b. ☐ Take it easy.
c. ☐ Rush.   d. ☐ Speak slowly.

3. What is not mentioned?

a. ☐ Commuting.   b. ☐ Fringe benefits.
c. ☐ Dividend.   d. ☐ Paycheck.

→ **Voir réponses page 108.**

PART 4 / TRAINING

You have reached a recording. Thank you for calling Westfarms Mall Cinema located on Connecticut route 71 Southwest of Hartford. We are pleased to offer you 3 films for your entertainment. *Ice Age 4* for kids will be shown at 4 pm every day till Sunday. *La La Land* the smash musical for all ages can be seen at 6 pm for 2 weeks. *Fifty Shades of Grey* forbidden for under 16 will be shown at 10 pm Saturday and Sunday.

This message will repeat but you can also find full movie listings and movie time schedules on:

www.westfarms.mallcinema.com.

Questions

1. How many films for all audiences will be shown?

a. ☐ 4.   b. ☐ 3.   c. ☐ 2.   d. ☐ None.

2. When can *Ice Age* be seen?

a. ☐ At 3 pm today.   b. ☐ Only on Sunday.
c. ☐ At 6 pm.   d. ☐ At 4 pm everyday.

3. What can you do to have more details?

a. ☐ Dial again.   b. ☐ Visit the cinema.
c. ☐ Visit the website.   d. ☐ Ask Connecticut.

→ **Voir réponses page 108.**

BestRide.com is a new website if you want to purchase used cars. The information that pops up for each listing is well detailed. There are nice photos for each vehicle. The site, overall, is pleasant to look at and easy to use. The search will direct you from the closest used cars to the most-distant ones within a maximum of 150 miles.

Once you have found a suitable car, the website will put you directly in contact with the dealership and will also give you the choice of calling the dealer directly but we recommend not doing so. Make sure you always go through us to avoid being bothered by dealership offers in the future.

Questions

1. What is BestRide.com?

a. ⭘ A site to book a ride.   **b.** ⭘ A site to buy new cars.

c. ⭘ A site to buy second hand cars.   **d.** ⭘ A site to learn how to ride.

2. How far can you go to get a car?

a. ⭘ 150 miles.   **b.** ⭘ 150 km.

c. ⭘ 50 miles.   **d.** ⭘ A hundred miles.

3. Why is it recommended not to phone the dealership first and foremost?

a. ⭘ It's dangerous.   **b.** ⭘ It's risky.   **c.** ⭘ The dealership may inundate you with offers.   **d.** ⭘ Not to be cheated.

→ **Voir réponses page 108.**

PART 4 / TRAINING / RÉPONSES

Réponses
training

1. b. **2.** d. **3.** a.

1. c. **2.** b. **3.** a.

1. c. **2.** d. **3.** c.

1. c. **2.** a. **3.** c.

Consigne

Voici la consigne telle que vous l'entendrez lors de la certification.

En conditions d'examen

 **1**
1. a.☐ b.☐ c.☐ d.☐
2. a.☐ b.☐ c.☐ d.☐
3. a.☐ b.☐ c.☐ d.☐

 **2**
1. a.☐ b.☐ c.☐ d.☐
2. a.☐ b.☐ c.☐ d.☐
3. a.☐ b.☐ c.☐ d.☐

 **3**
1. a.☐ b.☐ c.☐ d.☐
2. a.☐ b.☐ c.☐ d.☐
3. a.☐ b.☐ c.☐ d.☐

 **4**
1. a.☐ b.☐ c.☐ d.☐
2. a.☐ b.☐ c.☐ d.☐
3. a.☐ b.☐ c.☐ d.☐

 **5**
1. a.☐ b.☐ c.☐ d.☐
2. a.☐ b.☐ c.☐ d.☐
3. a.☐ b.☐ c.☐ d.☐

 **6**
1. a.☐ b.☐ c.☐ d.☐
2. a.☐ b.☐ c.☐ d.☐
3. a.☐ b.☐ c.☐ d.☐

 **7**
1. a.☐ b.☐ c.☐ d.☐
2. a.☐ b.☐ c.☐ d.☐
3. a.☐ b.☐ c.☐ d.☐

➜ **Voir réponses pages 113-118.**

PART 4 / EN CONDITIONS D'EXAMEN

1. a.☐ b.☐ c.☐ d.☐
2. a.☐ b.☐ c.☐ d.☐
3. a.☐ b.☐ c.☐ d.☐

Aide visuelle exercice 8

TIME	DESTINATION	FLIGHT	GATE	REMARKS
13:08	HONG KONG	K591	13	CANCELLED
13:24	NEW YORK	Y880	20	ON TIME
13:44	LONDON	N472	16	DELAYED
13:50	TOKYO	K140	33	ON TIME
14:02	BERLIN	R569	12	ON TIME
14:18	MADRID	D313	05	CANCELLED
14:24	SYDNEY	Y560	11	DELAYED
14:30	ST PETERSBURG	1917	36	DELAYED 2H

1. a.☐ b.☐ c.☐ d.☐
2. a.☐ b.☐ c.☐ d.☐
3. a.☐ b.☐ c.☐ d.☐

Aide visuelle exercice 9

AYURVEDIC MASSAGE
EVERY DAY FROM 13:00 TO 14:00

NEKO CAFE (2 new cats)
ANYTIME DURING OFFICE HOURS

YOGA CLASSES
OUTSIDE WORKING HOURS

1. a.☐ b.☐ c.☐ d.☐
2. a.☐ b.☐ c.☐ d.☐
3. a.☐ b.☐ c.☐ d.☐

➔ **Voir réponses pages 121-124.**

PART 4 / EN CONDITIONS D'EXAMEN / RÉPONSES

Réponses
de cette mise en conditions

Awareness of the importance of the preservation of the environment has been top of the agenda for more than half a century, though there is still a lot to do to change mindsets. To make it work, proof that ecology and economy go hand in hand must be provided.

Going green will pay off and companies must keep searching for breakthroughs and governments must offer more incentives to promote the adoption of hybrid-electric cars for example.

Teaching the young generations is essential too and environmental classes should be compulsory from primary schools to high schools.

Questions

1. How long has ecology been discussed?

a. For a century.   **b. For more than 50 years.**
c. Over the past 30 years.   d. Not been discussed yet.

2. What should companies do?

a. Stop searching.   **b. Be innovative.**   c. Offer promotions.
d. Encourage the use of hybrid-electric cars.

3. What should the schooling system do?

a. Adopt hybrid cars.   **b. Make ecology courses mandatory.**
c. Implement optional ecology courses.   d. Ignore ecology.

PART 4 / EN CONDITIONS D'EXAMEN / RÉPONSES

Hello Mr Boyd,

This is Jenny Morrison, human ressources manager of Xtra Company. I'm calling to tell you that we received your résumé as well as your cover letter. My colleagues and I have been very impressed by your credentials and I'm happy to announce that your application has been chosen for the accounting position.

I would like to schedule an interview next Thursday. Could you please contact me on the displayed number to arrange a time? I'm looking forward to meeting you.

Questions

1. Who most likely is Mr Boyd?

a. A manager.   **b.** A student.   **c. An accountant.**   **d.** A musician.

2. Why does the speaker call?

a. To tell Mr Boyd he failed.
b. To announce he is hired.
c. To arrange an interview.
d. To say they are sorry.

3. When will the interview take place?

a. Next Thursday.
b. Next Monday.
c. Next Tuesday.
d. At 3 pm.

Children who cannot afford the latest brands and fashions may face bullying and ridicule by their peers. Advertising and marketing have made our society increasingly image-conscious and our children are suffering the consequences. Schools and colleges should be places where all children feel equal. Parents are also put under heavy pressure because they don't want their children to be excluded so they're forced to spend money on expensive and varied wardrobes for their children. That's why wearing school uniforms is essential.

Questions

1. Why are children influenced to wear the latest fashion?

a. Because brands advertise a lot.
b. Because school uniforms are old fashioned.
c. Because the parents agree.
d. Because their peers are ridiculous.

2. What happens when children don't wear the key brand?

a. They are pestered by bullies.   b. They are accepted by their peers.
c. They go and buy some fashionable brands.   d. They feel equal.

3. Why wear a uniform?

a. Because it is expensive.
b. Because everybody is equal.
c. Because parents are poor.
d. Because it looks nice.

PART 4 / EN CONDITIONS D'EXAMEN / RÉPONSES

Good news for worried parents: all those hours their teenagers spend socializing on the Internet are not a bad thing, according to a new study by Living and Learning with the Media foundation.

Hanging out with social media gives teens the technological skills and literacy they need to succeed in the contemporary world. They learn how to get along with others, how to manage a public identity and how to create a home page. Parents are often concerned about predators and stranger danger but actually they shouldn't worry because they are mainly socializing with their friends and people they've met at school or through sports.

Questions

1. What is the good news?

a. Teenagers stop going on the Net.
b. Parents don't worry.
c. **The Internet is beneficial to teenagers.**
d. Teenagers sign out of the Internet.

2. What are the main benefits of social media?

a. Teenagers meet predators.
b. **Teenagers are prepared for the modern technologies.**
c. Teenagers waste time.   d. Teenagers are cleverer.

3. Who are they socializing with?

a. Predators.   b. Strangers.   c. Their neighbours.   d. **Their peers.**

Are you a shopping addict? Well it all takes place in your brain! Dopamine is one of the most addictive substances known to man and purchasing decisions are driven, in part, by its seductive effects. When you see that brand new shiny smartphone or those flashy earrings for example, dopamine subtly floods your brain with pleasure. Then it takes as little as 2.5 seconds to make a purchasing decision. A few minutes later as you exit the store, bag in hand, the euphoric feeling caused by the dopamine diminishes and all of a sudden you wonder whether it was the right thing to do. Sound familiar?

Questions

1. What is the main purpose of the talk?

a. **The effect of dopamine.**   b. Problems in our brain.
c. Purchasing habits.   d. Making a decision.

2. How long does it take to make a purchasing decision?

a. 2.5 minutes.   b. 2.5 hours.
c. **Only a few seconds.**   d. A lifetime.

3. Why does the speaker say "sound familiar?"?

a. Because we buy smartphones and earrings too.
b. **Because we all have dopamine.**
c. Because we never make impulsive purchases.
d. Because we know we have made a bad buy.

PART 4 / EN CONDITIONS D'EXAMEN / RÉPONSES

Thank you for listening to the traffic news. Construction work on the downtown mall is causing heavy traffic delays along Hudson Street making it difficult to reach the downtown area between the 8:30 am and 5:30 pm rush hours. Local authorities recommend taking alternative routes. Traffic controllers will be stationed along these roads during all the works. For further traffic information, please check our website.

Questions

1. What is the main topic of this report?

a. Advertisement about a new mall.

b. Information about traffic.

c. Works on alternative routes.

d. About rush hour.

2. Who will provide assistance to the drivers?

a. Mall workers.

b. Local authorities.

c. Traffic controllers.

d. Police officers.

3. What can you do to keep up to date?

a. Call the workers.

b. Visit the website.

c. Stop on the side of the road.

d. Ask a police officer.

PART 4 / EN CONDITIONS D'EXAMEN / RÉPONSES

Morning Ms Dooley,

This is Zoe from Bangs. I am calling to let you know that your hair stylist, Cindy, won't be able to take your appointment at 4pm tomorrow. I am sorry about the inconvenience but Cindy was not feeling well and had to make an appointment to see the doctor. I would be happy to reschedule your appointment with another hair stylist at the time of your original appointment or if you prefer, you can wait until next week when Cindy has recovered. Please could you call me back to tell me what will be best for you?

Questions

1. Where does the speaker work?

a. In a beauty shop.   **b. In a hair salon.**
c. At a stylist's.   **d.** At a home designer.

2. What's the problem with Cindy?

a. She was fired.
b. She quit.
c. She doesn't want to see Ms Dooley.
d. She is sick.

3. What option was not offered to Ms Dooley?

a. Have another hair stylist.
b. Wait for Cindy.
c. Have a discount.
d. Make another appointment.

PART 4 / EN CONDITIONS D'EXAMEN / RÉPONSES

Attention please. To all passengers waiting to board flight 1917 to St Petersburg. Your plane has been delayed due to snow in Russia. We don't expect it to land in London for another 2 hours so boarding won't take place until 14:30. We are sorry for the inconvenience and we'll keep you up to date.

May we remind you that our lounge will provide you all with food and drinks while you're waiting.

Questions

1. Where does the announcement take place?

a. On a ship.

b. In a train station.

c. At an airport.

d. On a ferry.

2. Why is there a delay?

a. There was a bomb threat.

b. Because of bad weather conditions.

c. Because of mechanical problems.

d. A passenger was unwell.

3. What are the passengers offered while waiting?

a. Food and drinks.   b. To go out.

c. To sleep.   d. Films.

Lilac Laboratories, one of the world's major pharmaceutical companies, announced that for the third year in a row it was selected as one of the 50 best companies to work for. Indeed Lilac Laboratories is very committed to employee health and fitness. People who work long hours deserve to be well looked after. That's why some free services are at the employees' disposal. From massage to yoga classes, from staff lounges to stroking cats and dogs, everything is done to boost productivity through well being.

Questions

1. Why was Lilac Laboratories selected?

a. **Because it is committed to its staff's well being.**
b. Because they work a lot.
c. Because they make good products.
d. Because it makes organic products.

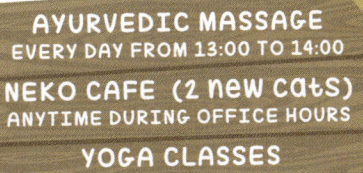

2. What can't the staff do?

a. Stroke pets.   b. Get a free massage.
c. **Go to the pool.**   d. Do yoga.

3. Why does Lilac Laboratories do this?

a. Because they love their staff.
b. **Because it boosts productivity.**
c. Because they love spending money.
d. Because it is a new fad.

PART 4 / EN CONDITIONS D'EXAMEN / RÉPONSES

First and foremost, I have an announcement. As you all know, this is my last board of directors meeting and I shall retire by the end of the year, after 20 years of good and loyal service.

I don't want to get emotional but I would like to thank you all for your cooperation all through the years. I would also like you to give a warm welcome to my worthy successor who you all know, Paul McDue.

I know he will be able to continue the work which has been undertaken for years by this company.

Now we shall proceed with the agenda.

Questions

1. What will the speaker do?

a. Go on holiday.   **b.** Find a replacement.
c. Get emotional.   **d. Retire.**

2. How long has he been working?

a. For 20 years.
b. Since 1997.
c. For ages.
d. A year.

3. What do we guess about his successor?

a. He is a new comer.
b. He is German.
c. He already works for the company.
d. He won't be good.

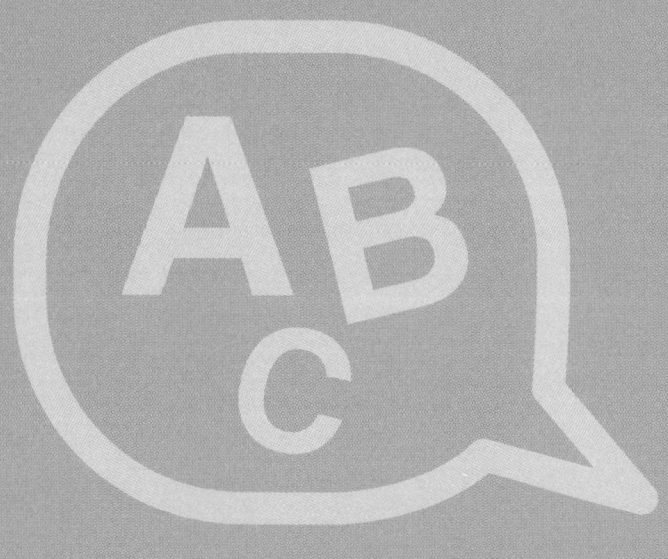

Glossaire

GLOSSAIRE

• World of work / le monde du travail

Allowance: une allocation

Bank holiday: un jour férié

Bonus: une prime

Compensation: une indemnité

Entitlements: avantages sociaux

Intern: un stagiaire

Internship: un stage

Job hunting: la recherche d'emploi

Job-seeker: un demandeur d'emploi

Layoff: un licenciement

Meal voucher: un ticket restaurant

Paid leave: congés payés

Parental leave: congé parental

Pension scheme: plan de retraite

Perks: avantages

Position / job: un poste

Probation: une période d'essai

Redundancies: licenciements

Retirement: la retraite

Reward: une récompense

Sick leave: congé maladie

To apply for a job: postuler à un emploi

To be fired: être congédié

To be hired / to be employed: être embauché

To be jobless / to be unemployed: être sans emploi

To be made redundant: être licencié

To be on the dole: être au chômage

To be short listed: présélectionné

To fit the job: convenir au poste

To get a job interview: obtenir un entretien d'embauche

To hire / to employ: embaucher

To lay off: licencier

To look for a job: chercher un emploi

To lose one's job: perdre son emploi

To match the profile: correspondre au profil

To match the requirements: satisfaire à la demande

To meet the expectations: répondre aux attentes

To retire: prendre sa retraite

To reward: récompenser

To seek a job: être à la recherche d'un emploi

To succeed in a job interview: réussir un entretien d'embauche

To take on: embaucher

Wages: salaire

Work overtime: faire des heures supplémentaires

• Jobs / les métiers

Accountant: un comptable

Adviser: un conseiller

Baker: un boulanger

Blue collar worker: un ouvrier, travailleur manuel

Broker: un courtier

Butcher: un boucher

Buyer: un acheteur

CEO / chief executive officer: un PDG

Chartered accountant: un expert-comptable

Civil servant: un fonctionnaire

Clerk: un employé de bureau

Contractor: un entrepreneur

Cook: un cuisinier

Deliveryman: un livreur

Executive: un cadre

Handler: un manutentionnaire

Junior executive: un cadre junior

Mechanic: un mécanicien

GLOSSAIRE

Representative: *un représentant*
Salesman: *un vendeur*
Senior executive: *un cadre supérieur*
Skilled worker: *un ouvrier qualifié*
Stewardess: *hôtesse de l'air*
Temporary worker: *un intermédiaire*
To be in charge of: *être en charge de*
To be responsible for: *être responsable de*
White collar worker: *employé de bureau*

• Sectors / les secteurs d'activité

Advertising: *publicité*
Banking: *banque*
Catering: *restauration*
Chemicals: *industrie chimique*
Computer industry: *industrie informatique*
Food and kindred products: *agroalimentaire*
Health: *la santé*
Hospitality: *hôtellerie*
Hotel business: *hôtellerie*
Iron and steel industry: *sidérurgie*
Leisure and tourism: *loisir et tourisme*
Luxury goods industry: *industrie du luxe*
Machinery: *machines-outils*
Pharmaceutical industry: *industrie pharmaceutique*
Primary, secondary, tertiary sectors: *secteurs primaire, secondaire, tertiaire*
Publishing: *édition*
Real estate: *immobilier*
Shipbuilding: *industrie navale*

• The firm / l'entreprise

Accounts departement: *service comptabilité*
Advertising departement: *service publicité*
Branch: *une succursale*
Chemical plant: *une usine chimique*
Factory: *une usine*
Firm: *une entreprise*
Head office: *siège social*
IT department: *service informatique*
Nuclear plant: *une centrale nucléaire*
Plant: *une centrale*
Power plant: *une centrale électrique*
Private limited company: *SARL*
Public limited company: *SA*
Research and development / R&D : *département de recherche et développement*
Subsidiary: *une filiale*
Venture: *une entreprise*

• The premises / les locaux

Assembly line: *une chaîne de montage*
Building: *un bâtiment*
Canteen: *la cantine*
Factory floor: *un atelier de production*
Parking lot: *un parking*
Post room / mail room: *le service courrier*
Switchboard: *le standard*
Warehouse: *un entrepôt*
Workshop: *un atelier*

• The secretariat / le secrétariat

Desk: *un bureau*

Diary: *un agenda*

To file: *classer*

File: *un dossier*

Folder: *un classeur*

To sort out: *archiver*

Office stationary / supplies: *fournitures de bureau*

Stapler: *une agrafeuse*

To be busy: *être occupé / avoir un emploi du temps chargé*

To make an appointment: *prendre un rendez-vous*

To put somebody through: *passer quelqu'un au téléphone*

• On a business trip / en voyage d'affaires

Accommodation: *un logement / une chambre*

Check in: *arriver dans un hôtel*

Check out: *quitter un hôtel*

Deposit: *un acompte*

Double bed: *un lit double*

Double bedrooms: *chambres doubles*

King / queen size bed: *un grand lit*

To book / to reserve: *réserver*

To make travel arrangements: *faire les préparatifs de voyage*

To overnight: *passer une nuit*

To pack: *faire ses bagages*

To unpack: *défaire ses bagages*

To rent a car: *louer une voiture*

Reservation fees: *frais de réservation*

• Banking / la banque

Bankrupcy: *une faillite*

Bear market: *un marché à la baisse*

Bill note: *un billet*

Bull market: *un marché à la hausse*

Currency: *une devise*

Interest rate: *un taux d'intérêt*

Invoice: *une facture*

Listed: *coté*

Loan: *un prêt*

Mortgage: *un prêt immobilier*

Non payment defaulting: *un défaut de paiement*

Overdraft: *avoir un découvert*

Profitable: *qui dégage des bénéfices*

Receipt: *un reçu*

Share: *une action*

Shareholder: *un actionnaire*

Stock exchange: *la Bourse*

Thriving / flourishing: *qui prospère*

To borrow money from: *emprunter*

To draw a cheque: *rédiger un chèque*

To go bankrupt: *faire faillite*

To go public: *entrer en Bourse*

To grant a loan: *accorder un crédit*

To lend: *prêter*

To make a profit: *faire des bénéfices*

Unlisted: *non coté*

TABLEAU D'AUTOÉVALUATION

Bravo, vous êtes venu à bout de ce cahier ! Il est temps à présent de faire le point sur vos compétences et de comptabiliser les icônes afin de procéder à l'évaluation finale. Reportez le sous-total de chaque partie dans les cases ci-dessous, puis additionnez-les afin d'obtenir le nombre final d'icônes dans chaque couleur. Enfin, découvrez vos résultats !

Part 1 Photographs ....

Part 2 Questions & responses ....

Part 3 Short conversations ....

Part 4 Short talks ....

Total, toutes parties confondues ....

Vous avez obtenu une majorité de...

Good job!
Vous pouvez vous présenter
à la certification !

Keep going…
Vous pouvez encore progresser ! Refaites les exercices qui vous ont donné du fil à retordre !

Don't give up!
Reprenez l'ensemble de l'ouvrage et comprenez vos erreurs.

CRÉDITS

Crédits iconographiques :

iStock : alexeyrumyantsev : 26bd, 29m ; andrei_r : 35hd, 39 exo 25 ; artbesouro : 114,119 ; Cecilie_Arcurs : 14bg, 18b ; dobok : 14hg, 18mb ; earl_of_omaha : 13bd,18hm ; estherpoon : 23h, 28hg ; Figure8Photos : 33hd, 38 exo 21 ; fiphoto : 24b, 28b ; gilaxia : 15bd,19hm, 27hd, 29bm ; g-stockstudio : 9, 13bd, 18hg ; Hramovnick : 35bd, 39 exo 26 ; intararit : 72 ; iphotographer : 37b, 39 ; jacoblund : 25hd, 29hg ; Juanmonino : 34hd, 38 exo 23 ; LuckyBusiness : 34bd, 38 exo 23 ; Maria Zainoullina : 118 ; MarianVejcik : 25bd, 29hg ; Mikolette : 16bg, 19bm ; Minerva Studio : 26hg, 29hg ; Mladen_Kostic : 27bd, 29b ; narvikk : 17bd,19h ; Qvasimodo : 76 ; Rasica : 17dg, 19b ; Rawpixel : 37hd, 39 exo 29 ; romrodinka : 36b, 39 exo 28 ; RyanJLane : 24g, 28bm ; shironosov : 16hg,19m ; TCmake_photo : 103 ; VidojkovicART : 33bd, 38 exo 22 ; wongkaer : 36hd, 39 exo 27 ; xavierarnau : 15hd, 19 ; zhudifeng : 23b, 28hm ; **Shutterstock :** Altagracia Art : 89 ; AriSys : 81 ; Blablo101 : 82 ; Chernoskutov Mikhail : 44hd ; Fay Francevna : 63 ; Fred Ho : 67 ; graphic-line : 79 ; gst : 65 ; Henry Olden : 45m ; Iconic Bestiary : 59 ; Iconic Bestiary : 73, 75 ; Incomible : 106 ; jesadaphorn : 45b, 46, 71, 74 ; Julia Tim : 116 ; Lindarks : 91 ; Macrovector : 49, 90, 97 ; Marharyta Pavliuk : 98 ; Maria Zainoullina : 83 ; Marish : 21h ; Mascha Tace : 5, 77, 92 ; Millena : 84 ; Olga1818 : 44, 117 ; Padma Sanjaya : 113 ; Petrovic Igor : 21d ; Rudie Strummer : 43 ; S.Noree Saisalam : 108 ; Seita : 57 ; Tanya_Knyazeva : 66 ; Tomacco : 51 ; watchtaxinyc : 21g ; yuriytsirkunov : 105 ; **Vecteeezy :** ancientartonya : 96 ; FlipperD2 : 107 ; getfile : 95 ; joezhuang : 88, 95 ; Maria Zainoullina : 122 ; nightwolfdezines : 80 ; Vetreno : 31g ; watchtaxinyc : 115 ; yellowlion120 : 94 ; zhaolifang : 87, 93, 112,120 ; Olga1818 : 72-73.

Création et réalisation : Lunedit, lunedit.com
Couverture : Allright
Ingénieur du son :
Léonard Mule @ Studio du Poisson Barbu

© 2018, Assimil
Dépôt légal : avril 2018
N° d'édition : 3747
ISBN : 978-2-7005-0818-5

www.assimil.com

Imprimé en Slovénie par DZS Grafik